Bb BASS CLARINET

CONCERT FAVORITES

Volume 1

Band Arrangements Correlated with Essential Elements Band Method Book 1

ISBN 978-0-634-05204-0

HAL•LEONARD®

7777 W. BLUEMOUND RD. P.O. BOX 13819 MILWAUKEE, WI 53213

00860124

LET'S ROCK!

Bb BASS CLARINET

MICHAEL SWEENEY (ASCAP)

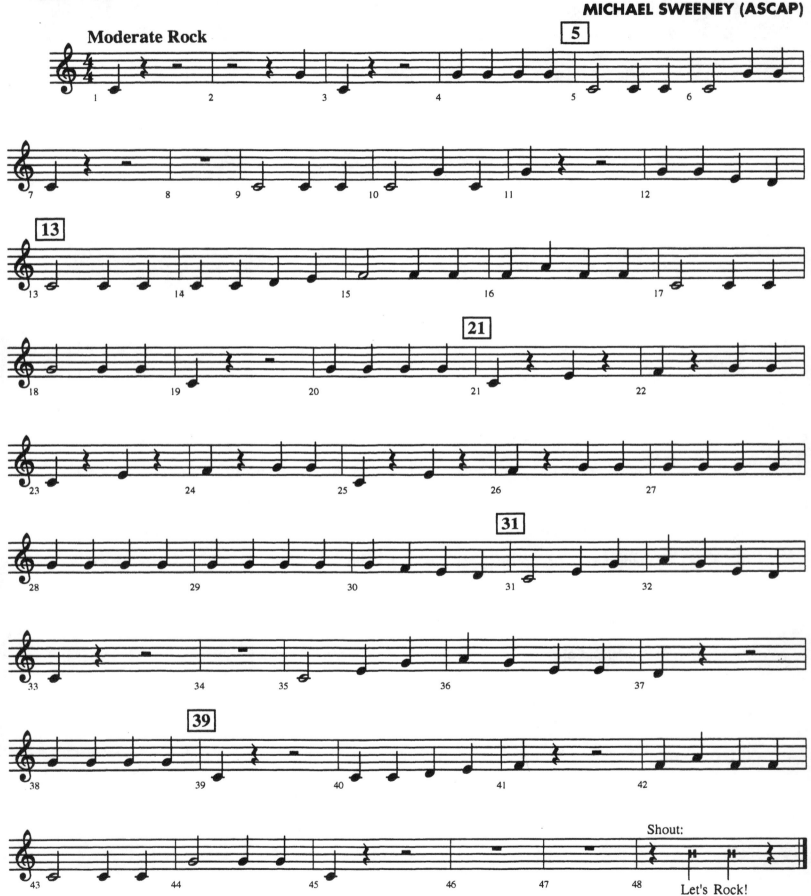

00860124

MAJESTIC MARCH

B♭ BASS CLARINET

By PAUL LAVENDER

March Tempo

00860124

MICKEY MOUSE MARCH
(From Walt Disney's "THE MICKEY MOUSE CLUB")

Bb BASS CLARINET

Words and Music by JIMMIE DODD
Arranged by MICHAEL SWEENEY

March Tempo

00860124

POWER ROCK

(We Will Rock You • Another One Bites The Dust)

Bb BASS CLARINET

Arranged by MICHAEL SWEENEY

WHEN THE SAINTS GO MARCHING IN

Words by KATHERINE E. PURVIS
Music by JAMES M. BLACK
Arranged by JOHN HIGGINS

Bb BASS CLARINET

March Style

FARANDOLE
(From "L'Arlésienne")

Bb BASS CLARINET

GEORGES BIZET
Arranged by MICHAEL SWEENEY (ASCAP)

00860124

JUS' PLAIN BLUES

Bb BASS CLARINET

MICHAEL SWEENEY (ASCAP)

From the Paramount and Twentieth Century Fox Motion Picture TITANIC

MY HEART WILL GO ON

(Love Theme From 'Titanic')

Music by JAMES HORNER
Lyric by WILL JENNINGS
Arranged by PAUL LAVENDER

B♭ Bass Clarinet

00860124

From THE MUPPET MOVIE

THE RAINBOW CONNECTION

Words and Music by PAUL WILLIAMS
and KENNITH L. ASCHER
Arranged by PAUL LAVENDER

Bb BASS CLARINET

00860124

From Walt Disney's MARY POPPINS

SUPERCALIFRAGILISTICEXPIALIDOCIOUS

Words and Music by
RICHARD M. SHERMAN and ROBERT B. SHERMAN
Arranged by MICHAEL SWEENEY

B♭ Bass Clarinet

00860124

(From "THE SOUND OF MUSIC")
DO-RE-MI

Bb BASS CLARINET

Lyrics by OSCAR HAMMERSTEIN II
Music by RICHARD RODGERS
Arranged by PAUL LAVENDER

Brightly

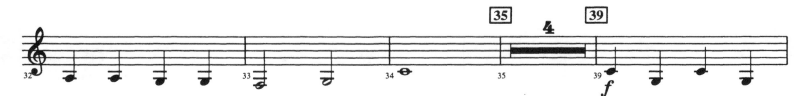

00860124

DRUMS OF CORONA

B♭ BASS CLARINET

MICHAEL SWEENEY (ASCAP)

00860124

LAREDO
(Concert March)

Bb BASS CLARINET

JOHN HIGGINS

00860124

POMP AND CIRCUMSTANCE
March No. 1

Bᵇ **BASS CLARINET**

By EDWARD ELGAR
Arranged by MICHAEL SWEENEY

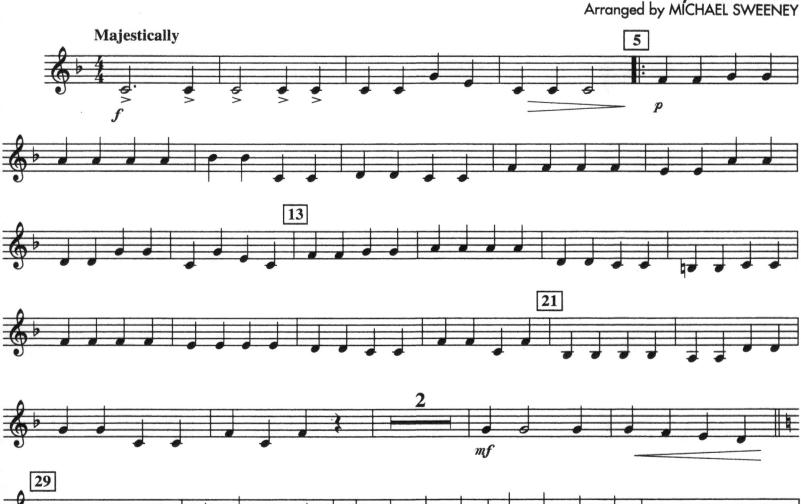

STRATFORD MARCH

B♭ BASS CLARINET

JOHN HIGGINS (ASCAP)